Trues Bridge,
Union. Me.
Trues Bridge,
Union. Me.
Trues Bridge,
Union. Me.
Trues Bridge,
Union. Me.

David Shaub

WITH RUTH E SHAW

BRIDGES to the Past

Union, Maine

Union Historical Society, 2003

Members of the Union Historical Society are pleased to support this effort.

Significant support has been gratefully received through a grant from MBNA America, Maine Grants Program.

Thanks to *Cameographics Publications* for donation of time and talents for the creation of this book. *www.cameographics.com*

Many of the homes and farms included in this book are privately owned. We ask that this privacy be respected.

Union Historical Society
343 Common Road
PO Box 154
Union Maine 04862

www.midcoast.com/comespring

ISBN 0-9678716-1-1

Library of Congress Control Number: 2003115693

Printed at JS McCarthy, Augusta, Maine

Contents

Acknowledgments

The Union Historical Society officers are pleased to bring this new collection of Union photographs to you. The UHS curators and Richard Tracy under the direction of Dorothy Davis have assembled and organized these and many other photographs. Todd Caverly has begun a process to record images of architectural details inside and outside of Union buildings. Members and visitors have helped to identify and comment upon many pictures. Arley Clark's research on Union schools allowed the photographs here to be displayed in some context. Harriet and David Carroll, John and Barbara Moody, and Muriel Heath have shared photographs and recollections, stories that they heard from past times. The 1909 William Bessey photograph of the framing of the giant barn is used through the kindness of the Maine Historical Preservation Commission, Augusta.

Marlene Groves has advised us along the way. The staff at J. S. McCarthy has been exemplary in its personal assistance and scheduling of the printing.

Ruth Shaw of Cameographics has supplied her considerable skills for layout and photograph preparation. This book could not have been done without her.

Union's many citizens over nearly 230 years deserve the greatest credit. It was, and is, they who have cleared land, built and rebuilt, and have cared enough to take pictures and to share them.

Dave Shaub

2003

Introduction

The historical novel *Come Spring* was published first in 1940. Ben Ames Williams, a frequent visitor to this part of Maine, did his research for the book painstakingly. He carefully read Sibley's *A History Of Union, Maine* (1851) and histories of near-by towns. He walked the roads and woods, and paddled the waterways. What emerged was a grand view of a small place. And he made that place, peopled with ordinary folks, a very special one indeed. The novel is a collection of real people's lives, connected as best he could in the guise of fiction.

But *Come Spring* is not fiction. And, people here in the 1770s and 1780s needed to do what everyone else has needed to do in the meantime: take care of one another in this place. These ordinary people are the heroes of real life, everyday happenings.

The incidents go on. In the eye of the Big World almost all are "incidental," of little consequence. Outside of families, many people's contributions are poorly known or worse, lost.

Yet all towns have collectors, people who save the stories and pass them on. Some have pictures of how life was, and who did what, and who was related to whom. Some collectors have whole buildings that have survived years and reflect the town's changes. Sometimes, lack of change.

This little book is an attempt to celebrate again our heritage in Union, focusing on the period between the publishing of *200 Years In Union* in 1974 and the present, 2003. To do so, previously unpublished photographs from Union's past are used along with ones taken within these years. The quotations found at the beginnings of most sections are taken from *Come Spring*, the 1st Edition and the Union Historical Society's 2000 Edition.

Enjoy it.

Union's Recent History

Being here, even for a day, provides a memorable experience; picturesque places are dotted with buildings, dotted even more finely with people. Waterways move through pretty much as they have for a very long time.

Official Town Reports and records provide a more statistical view of life as it was and is, and they record plans and accomplishments.

That casual visitor finds a town that "feels old." There are enough old buildings to remind many adults of "grandmother's place." Indeed numerous old houses here do contain grandmothers. The open spaces contribute to the sense of spaciousness so rapidly being diminished in much of the world, including Maine. The ponds, lakes, and flowing water are tucked among old hills. The place seems to possess an unreal Brigadoon-like quality, or to be a Norman Rockwell site.

But anyone who's stayed around even a short time will find a population of people living very much in this time. People are born, and others die. Businesses flourish; businesses wither. Someone plants the fields, tends the animals, stocks the shelves, preaches the sermons, delivers the fuel. This isn't make-believe and it shouldn't stay as it is; things must change.

Following the generation described in *Come Spring* in the late 1700s, Union's population grew. It grew until about 1850, when over 1800 people lived here, centered around the somewhat-separate villages of North Union, East Union, South Union, and Union Village. The Civil War and the "discovery" of rich farmlands and cities to the West reduced Maine's largely-agricultural populations significantly. It was not until the 1980s that the population of Union again reached that number. In 2003 there are well over 2200.

Numerous important changes occurred since our local Bicentennial in 1974. That year the town received the Grand Award through the Maine Community Betterment Drive. Robert Heald contributed the instantly-famous birdhouse road signs, at first making and caring for them by himself. Under Bob's leadership, the tennis and basketball courts were built, still a bit of a surprise to see in a small town, and still well-maintained by citizen committees. When Bob Heald died he left a generous fund that continues to support youth scholarships, the recreation program, the Vose Library, the Methodist church, and the local "country club." (Again, he had developed the golf course.) Route 17, the newer one built in the 1950s, is aptly named "Heald Highway."

Ayer Park, a jewel of a small town's public park was improved. The year was 1974. The years immediately following saw the transfer of the Thompson Building and the Yellow School to the town from what's become School Administrative District #40. A new Union Elementary School and D.R. Gaul Middle School were built on a commodious lot on Route 17. Streets were asphalted; spraying of tar over gravel was discontinued. The town focused on town offices, and finally a new Town Office and Fire Department/Ambulance Building opened in 1987. A combination of the Pullens' generous endowments and the approval by the local taxpayers produced an enviable facility. As many communities have done in the recent past, Union struggled with issues of waste management, eventually closing the long-used town dump and joining the Tri-County Solid Waste organization.

Only in the early 1990s did the town move from a selectmen- administered government to a town manager form, recognizing increasing needs to have a full-time professional work with selectmen and with agencies in other towns. Code enforcement officers and assessors joined Union's town government, time-shared with other small towns. In spite of increasing duties, these and equally-dedicated clerks, treasurers, and road crews have managed the town's affairs well.

Emergencies such as the Great Ice Storm in the winter of 1997-1998 and the emergence of traffic concerns and street sign updating have come and gone. Two prominent buildings on Union Common burned, one in 1997 (the Masonic Hall) and one in 2002 (the Odd Fellows Hall). Local and area fire-fighters were heroic in both cases to contain the fires, tragic as the losses were. The new Common Market is testimony to Union's resilience. These and other more ordinary things done by regular people have kept the town going along.

The changes brought by more people, many of them coming from communities far away, continue. Will Union remain the same as it "always has been"? No. And, it never did remain the same as it had been. However, we who are here now have responsibility for making Union what it is and what it will become next.

Generations of people have lived here and have used the land. Hundreds, likely thousands, have served as volunteers in organizations and departments. The condition of the town and its attractiveness testify eloquently that they have done their work well. Enjoy these images of past and present places, and perhaps recall people who brought it to this time through their efforts. The old phrase, "Come Spring," reminds us that there are always opportunities ahead to do good things together.

Rivers

*"I like the river sliding by. A river's alive, I guess.
Before anybody came here, the river was right here."*

(143)

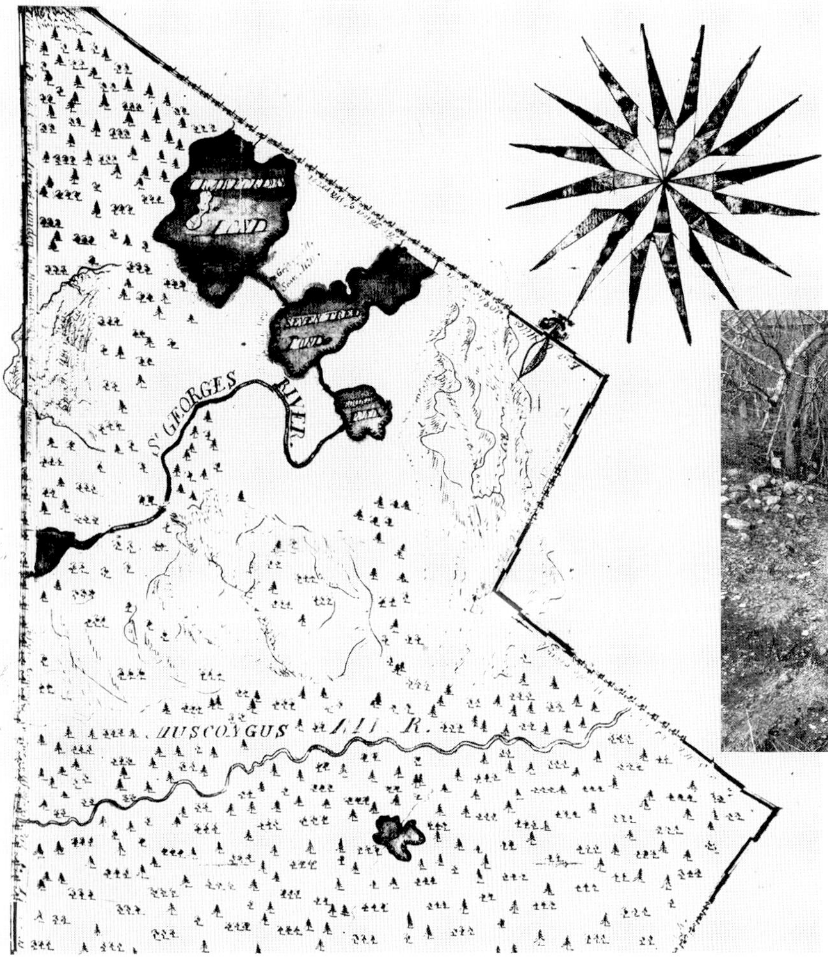

The 1700s map shows Union to be waterways and woods.

Union's rivers and lakes begin as little streams. Overlock Hill. 2003

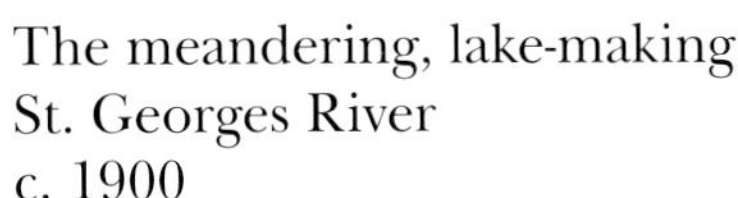

The meandering, lake-making St. Georges River c. 1900

Here, the St. Georges River connects Seven Tree Pond and Round Pond.
c. 1910

The scene shows a great deal of land, but water dominates.
c. 1910

The hills contain the water while others direct it as it moves.
c. 1900

The aerial view accentuates the trail of the St. Georges River. The oval is Union Fair's racetrack.
c. 1930

Surrounded by the beginnings of Union, Round Pond is still skirted by open and farm land.
c. 1913

True's bridge at the St. Georges River's opening into Seven Tree Pond.
c. 1930

We are almost able to count seven trees on the little island.
c. 1920

Recently preserved by a new dam, the lake provides miles of beautiful shoreline.
c. 1900

Much of this pond's shoreline is protected.
c. 1920

Quiet "usualness" is interrupted by remarkable natural oddities.
c. 1920

Occasionally, our waterways overflow, sometimes with disastrous results.
1936

Dams were built to control and to use the power of water. Hills Mills.
c. 1910

How did they accomplish so much hard work?
c. 1910

A new dam at Sennebec's southern end seems effective and inconspicuous.
2003

South Union's numerous factories relied on water flowing down from Crawford Pond.
c. 1890 and c. 1920

In the center of South Union.
c. 1920

(The large store was moved at night so as not to offend a neighbor who had refused to allow it to be moved across the land.)

A quiet mill pond with force and power as it pours away.
c. 1930

Still a place to relax, Ayer Park is just beyond the bridge on the left.
c. 1930

Pathways

"It's queer how quick even one man will make a path...pretty soon there's a road."

(696)

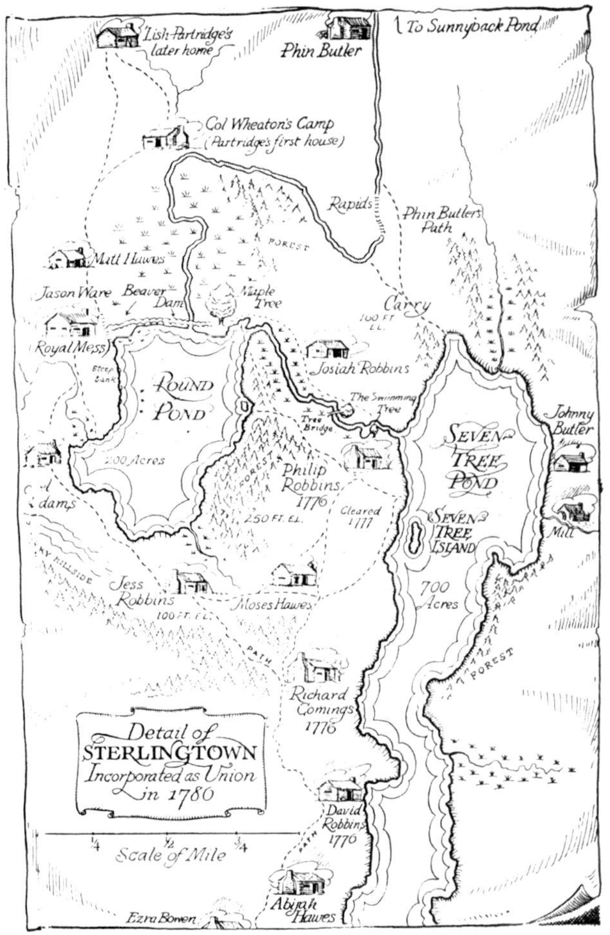

Sterlingtown Map

People and pathways came and did become roads. c. 1910

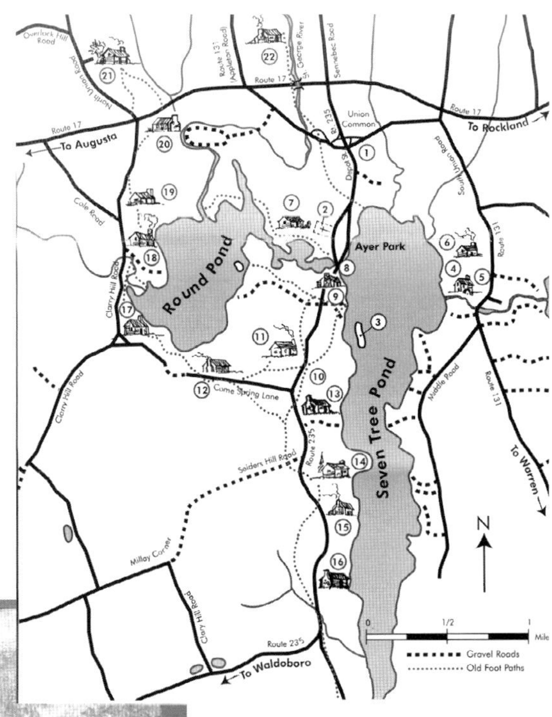

The Union Historical Society tour map. 2000

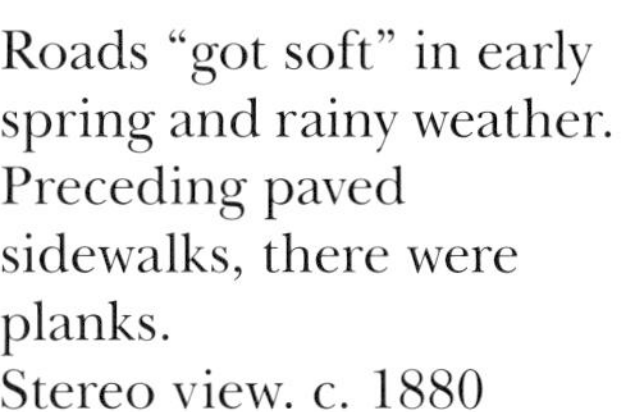

Roads "got soft" in early spring and rainy weather. Preceding paved sidewalks, there were planks.
Stereo view. c. 1880

Still a pleasant drive or walk down, and up, Common Road to town from the east.
c. 1910

A view back up the hill to the east.
c. 1910

Working out the rocks on Common Road.
c. 1900

Looking east from the Common. The Robbins House is on the right. c. 1890

Seven Tree Brook crosses Common Road. c. 1900

Heading up Ayer Hill Road.
c. 1900

Coming into Union Village on Depot Street, then called Elm Street.
c. 1910

Near the blueberry factory on Depot Street.
c. 1900

The mill building in the center is now passed by the bridge on the other side.
c. 1900

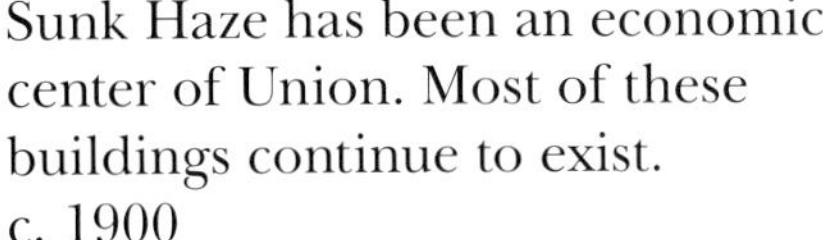

Sunk Haze has been an economic center of Union. Most of these buildings continue to exist.
c. 1900

The newer bridge into the Union Common.
c. 1935

South Union's pathways reflect its busy-ness.
c. 1900

The building at the right is on the site of Founders Park.
c. 1920

Going north among great elms. Sennebec Road and the Sibley place.
c. 1890

Houses accumulate along the pathways. At the left, Seven Tree Grange.
c. 1910

Common Road?
c. 1910

Roads must be made to last in spite of Maine winters. This may be South Hope's store.
c.1900

Still the crossroads in Union Village.
c. 1900

Unpaved roads still welcome us in springtime, if we make effort.
2003

Cars brought more demands on roads and for roads.
c. 1925

Georges Valley Railroad included freight and passenger cars. What great rolling stock.
c. 1910

Our "Union Station," off Depot Street near today's blueberry factory.
c. 1910

In a few weeks things may be mobile again, wood-powered.
1936

Mud and snow make work out of labor-saving transportaion.
c. 1915

Coming home to Union in spring is a beautiful thing.
c. 1920

Clearing

"It was as though by levelling the forest, men broke bonds which hemmed them here."
(212)

"Maybe some day trees will be scarce and folks will want to save them; but there's more trees than there's any sense to now."
(207)

A tangle of woods has become our towns and fields.

Evidence of the forest giants may still be found.
2003

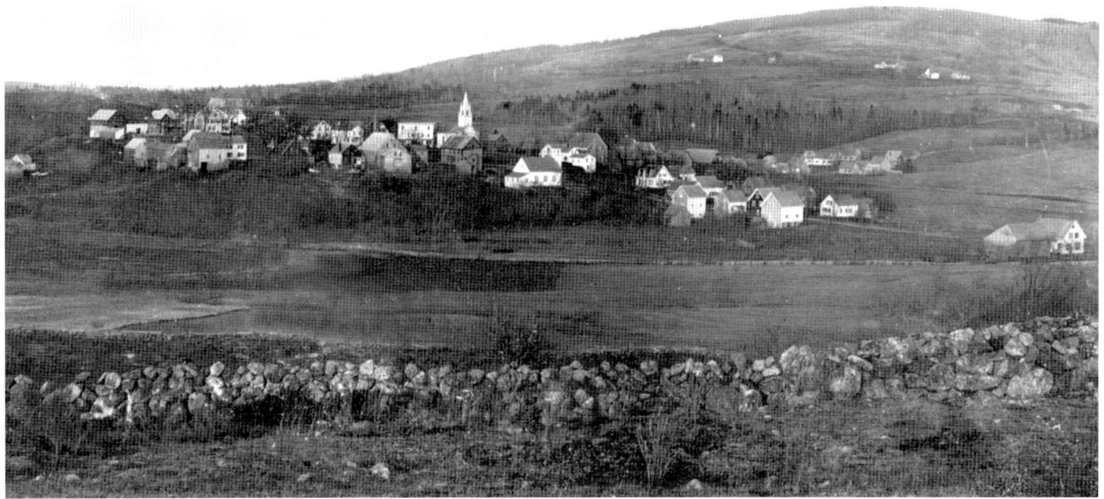

The forests are given over to pasture and cultivation. Union Village.

c. 1920

UNION, MAINE.

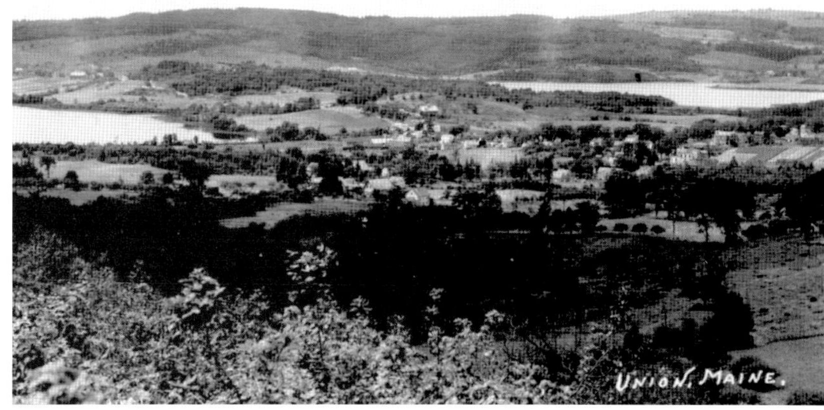

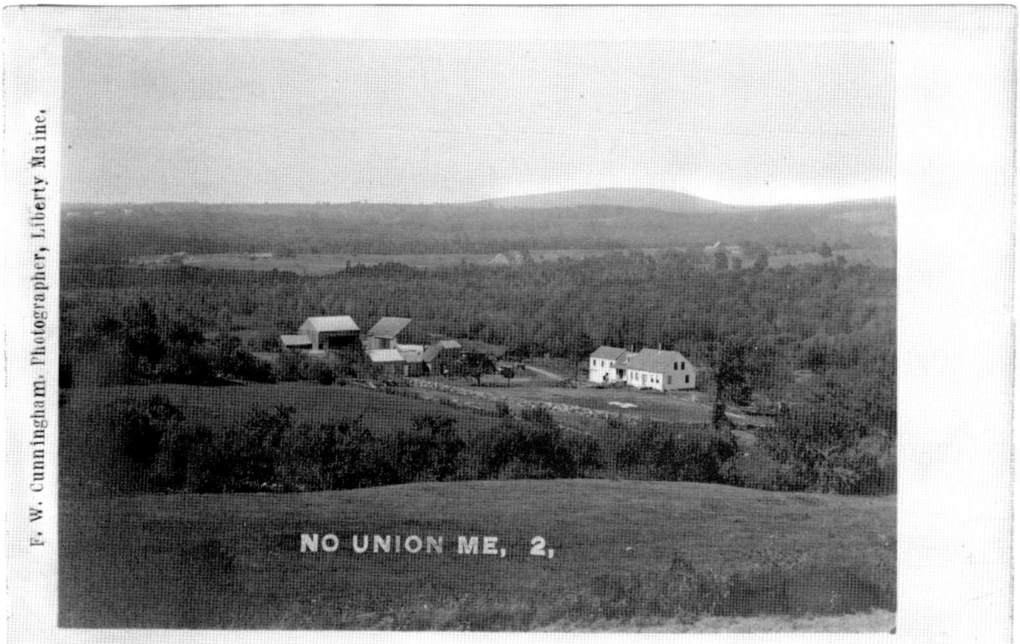
F. W. Cunningham. Photographer, Liberty Maine.
NO UNION ME, 2,

Scattered woods were allowed to return.

South Union with openness. South Union Road. c. 1900

So many fields.

Then, so much growing-back. 2003

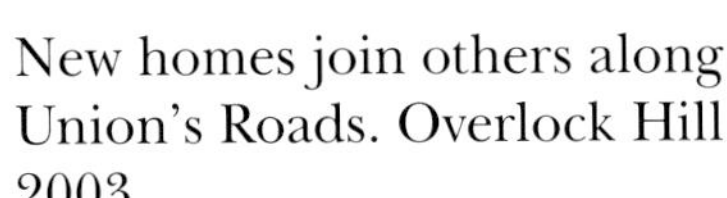

New homes join others along Union's Roads. Overlock Hill. 2003

Houses

"The new house stood back from the pond..."

(440)

"In the house there were, as always, meals to be prepared, and eaten, and cleaned up after; there was Polly to be kept clean and fed and happy; there was the floor to sweep; and..."

(816)

Depot Street's site of Philip Robbins' house up, away from the pond.
c. 1890 and 2003

This Clarry Hill Road home is on the site of *Come Spring's* Matthias Hawes' home.
c. 1960 and 2002

Ezra Bower built further down Seven Tree Pond from the Robbins' place.
Depot Street.
2001

A venerable, beautifully shaded house.
c. 1940

Ebenezer Alden came to Union in 1795, opened the first store, and remained. Common Road.
c. 1970

Common Road (left) South Union Road (right). Alden certainly continued his trade of finish (trim) carpentry.

East Union's bridge with the mill at the right.
c. 1890

This is seen with a new roofline just right of center above. This was the post office for a while.
c. 1960

By the mill pond in East Union, remains of early stencil work have been found.
2001

Daniels Road.
c. 1900 and 2001

South Union's cluster of lovely houses.
c. 1920

Once hip-roofed, this home is a South Union landmark.
c. 1910

Note that the door to the left is not in the center. An old barn has been added at the right.
c. 1965

South Union's cape
style house still stands
on Brown's Lane.
c. 1900

A superb old federal style house in South Union.
c. 1890, c. 1940 and 2002

Another wonderful federal house in South Union, preserved in its early form.
c. 1950 and 2001

Built in 1856. It's not hard to guess where the stairway is.
2002

A definitive Greek Revival home. South Union Road.
2002

Then and now on South Union Road.
c. 1910 and 2003

Two very rare stereo views of the same house, and that house today. South Union Road. c. 1880 and 2002

Looking west across the early 1900s bridge in Sunk Haze with an original duplex building at your right.
c. 1890

The stately duplex is further from the bridge today.
c. 2001

The same duplex is in the center. The new bridge now passes to the right of the mill building shown behind the bridge iron work.
c. 1920

Union's single example of Queen Anne style, c. 1890, remains prominent on the Common.
2002

Members of the Creighton family are photographed by their home on Common Road.
c. 1890

Several particularly well-maintained homes dominate the approach to the Common from the east.
2001

Thought to have been part of the big house on the Common, the former home of Union's Ed Matthews sits proudly on Common Road. c. 1950 and 2001

Converted to Union's only Gothic Revival home, this Common Road home once had a fancy portico with an iron railing on the roof. Even today, its front windows have their borders of stained glass.
2003 and c. 1920

Common Road homes easily recognized.

c. 1920

c. 1910

c. 1950

A wonderful home with its ell and barn on Depot Street.
2002

Going south on Depot Street.
c. 1910

A superb country Greek Revival dormer.
Depot Street.
2003

Appleton Road at a corner which had businesses since the early 1800s. 2002

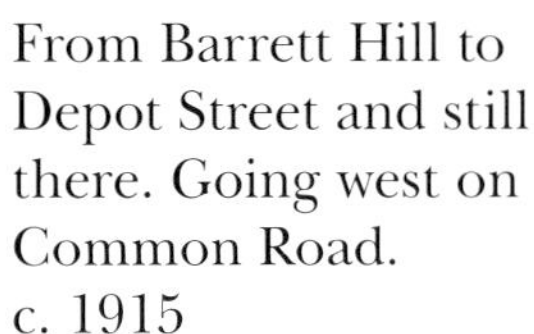

From Barrett Hill to Depot Street and still there. Going west on Common Road. c. 1915

The Bessey (Bessie) house. At first (c. 1830), a one story home. The second level was added early. Common Road. 2003

The old Thurston Place on North Union Road - half of the old double barn is at 630 South Union Road now. The owner is descended from Phinehas Butler.
c. 1930

Constructed in the 1790s this home still has a superb view down from North Union Road.
c. 1955(2) and 2001

This gable end defines part of the original Carroll (Cariel) place on North Union Road.
2003

Boasting what may be Union's finest doorway, this home is in North Union.
c. 1960 and 2002

A full two story colonial home may be seen at the base of Coggin Hill Road.
c. 1900

Hidden at the end of Upham Lane, these buildings, though modified, remain.
c. 1910

This Sennebec Road home was rebuilt by friends and neighbors after a fire in the 1930s.
2003

Few changes have occurred to this place which overlooks Sennebec Pond. Sennebec Road.
c. 1950 and 2003

This Carroll Road home had been modified and enlarged, and continues to have a spectacular view to the west.
c. 1910, 2002

Farms and Barns

"Talking won't make it ours...
We've got to use the land everywhere."

(10)

"All we had to eat was in it. We'll starve this winter."
(179)

" busy with the barn frame...end posts were raised
and the cross beams set piece by piece"
(307)

Early barns share the "English Pattern" with doors on the eave sides. Sennebec Road.
2002

South Union Road.
2002

Wotton Mill Road.
2003

South Union Road.
2002

One of Union's oldest big barns is on Clarry Hill Road up above Round Pond.
2003

Beautiful, but not identified.
c. 1950

The Hawes farm barns were, and are, amazing.
c. 1900, 2003

South Union Road.
2003

On Union Common!
2003

On the East Union Mill Pond.
2003

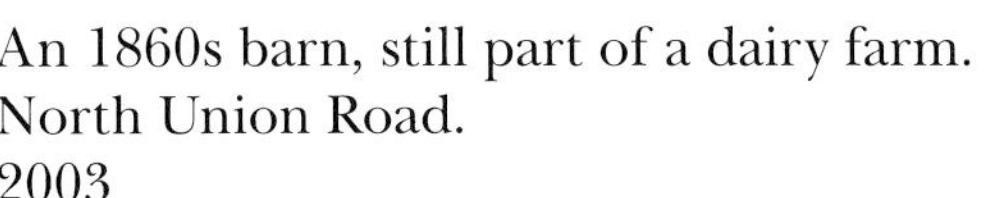

An 1860s barn, still part of a dairy farm.
North Union Road.
2003

A small barn remains standing square and level.
Sennebec Road.
2003

The afternoon light on this small barn glistens.
Barrett Hill Road.
2003

Do you see where the side bay was added to an old barn?
Wotton Mill Road.
2002

This small barn has accumulated an array of sheds and add-ons, as many have. Mt. Pleasant Road.
2003

These run-ins along the south side are extraordinary survivors. Heald Highway.
2002

"The Thompson Place" is shown from across Sennebec Pond. Augustin Thompson invented Moxie. Appleton Road. c. 1920

Locate this wonderful little shop building in the photo above. 2003

Outbuildings are made for specific functions.
Payson Road.
2003

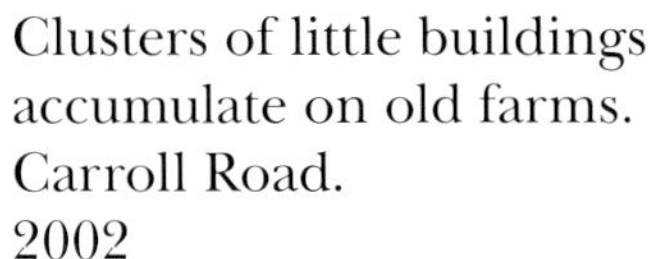

Clusters of little buildings accumulate on old farms.
Carroll Road.
2002

This little 19th century cobbler's shop was saved from demolition.
North Union Road.
2003.

The former residents, chickens, had a wonderful view. Carroll Road.
2003.

Outhouses and other outbuildings often were right on the ground and rotted away. This is a rare survivor. Clarry Hill Road. 2002

A new outhouse looks like a mighty chilly place. Common Road. 2003

This Bessey photo gives one some idea of size and of the work involved. It stands today on improved foundations. Clarry Hill Road. 1909 and 2003

Dutch-gable barn in midwest style (doors at the gable ends) provide extra loft space. Heald Highway. 2002

Davis Road. 2002

Miller Road. 2003

Few barns were built in Union in late 1800s styles. Common Road. 2002

As the house was enlarged in the 1800s, the old English-style barn has been supplemented by a 20th century one. Wotton Mill Road. 2003

A real working farm requires large areas under cover. Overlock Hill Road.
2003

An extra-large English style barn enjoys expansive views from North Union Road.
2002

Schools and Churches

"We ought to have a school ... and preaching, too."
(722)

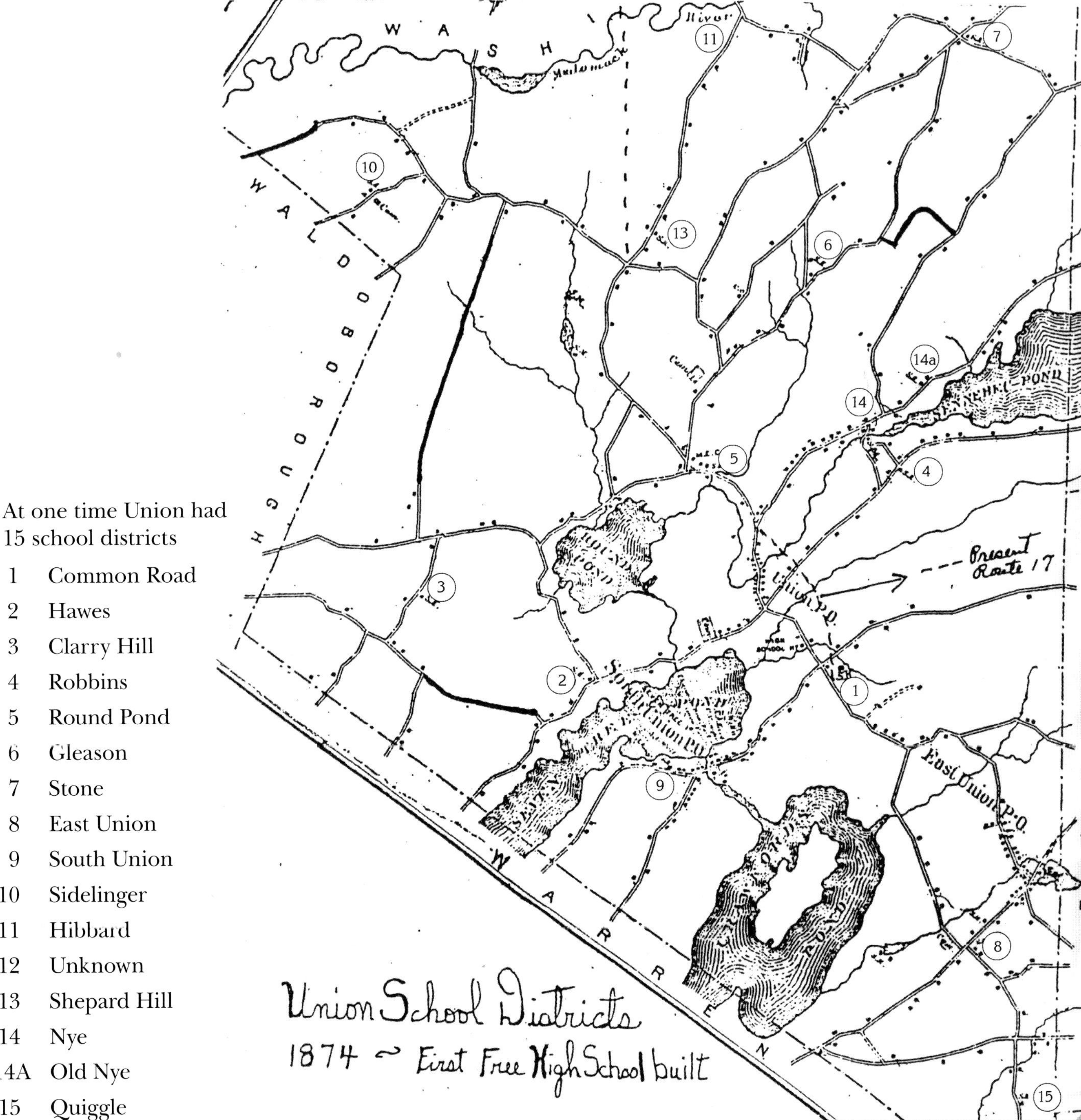

At one time Union had 15 school districts

1 Common Road
2 Hawes
3 Clarry Hill
4 Robbins
5 Round Pond
6 Gleason
7 Stone
8 East Union
9 South Union
10 Sidelinger
11 Hibbard
12 Unknown
13 Shepard Hill
14 Nye
14A Old Nye
15 Quiggle

Clarry Hill School. District 3.
c. 1900

District 9.
c. 1910

The Nye School, 14. It is now also a residence.
2002

Formerly the Nye School, 14a.
2003

Shepard Hill School, 1882. District 13.
2000 and 2002

East Union School, 1887. District 15.
2002

The Hawes School was moved north a few hundred yards and is enveloped in this home. District 2.
2003

North Union School, now a residence undergoing careful renovation, served District 11.
2003

South Union School

Back Row: Miles Leach, Norman Hannan, Theodore Sijli, Harvard Chandler, William Young, Carleton Robbins, Bruno Aho.

Front Row: Dorothy Young, Edward Young, Bernard Hannan, Taylor Twins, Catherine (?) Chandler

Back Row (Left to Right): Elston MacFarland, Jessie Pierce, George Cummings, Mabel Newbert, James Moody, Arlene Cummings, Harry Burns, Murry Simmons, Miss Helen Ripley.

Middle Row: Ernest Cunningham, Bertha Newbert, Richard Gorden, Mildred Farris, William Mank, Doreathea Hannan, Carl Cunningham, Edna Hannan, Carrie Prescott

Front Row: Bernard Esancy, unknown, unknown, and Maynard Pierce

Old Union Grade School
c. 1923

Round Pond School has evolved into an attractive residence. District 5. c. 1960, 2003

Union's Common School began north of present Heald Highway. In 1874 this building was built to house that school and Union's first high school. It was located about where the present fire department is. District 1. c. 1915

From 1932 to 1987 this was Union's school. Now preserved as part of Union's Community Center, it continues as a place of learning.
c. 1940, 2003

Union Elementary and D.R. Gaul Middle School occupy this building on Heald Highway.
2003

The Hodge School was moved to the Union fairgrounds to complement the Matthews Museum collections. It is worthy of a visit.
2002

The first Methodist church, 1810, was erected near the west end of Common Road.
c. 1870

The Methodists built this chapel in 1871, recognizing that a building in the center of the village would better serve.
c. 1880

Sold in 1902 and replaced by the present People's United Methodist Church, the chapel became a business building further south on Depot Street.
c. 1905

Since 1902 this attractive building has been the home of Union's Methodists. Its interior is a spectacular splash of original tin-work.
c. 1920

This church, built in the 1830s, dominated the Common from a site on its north side. c. 1910

The bell was reused at the present Methodist Church and the building converted to a store. c. 1915, c. 1920

The Congregational Church, built in 1839, sat at the east entrance to the Common area. c. 1910

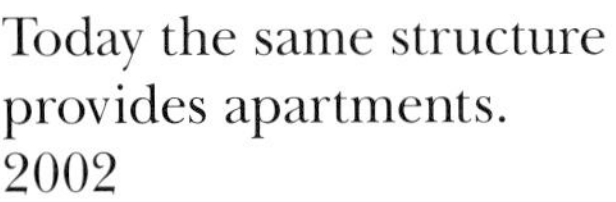

Today the same structure provides apartments. 2002

Services were held in the North Union Chapel as early as 1899. It is now a residence. North Union Road. 2002

The Chapel's congregation reorganized and built this church on South Union Road. It is now a business building. 1968

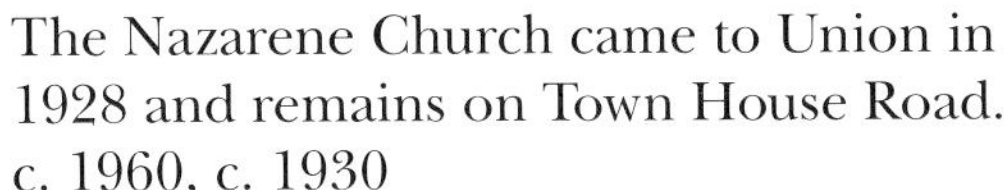

The Nazarene Church came to Union in 1928 and remains on Town House Road. c. 1960, c. 1930

Restoration and Reuse

"It'll always be ours, because we...first loved it."

(193)

"My barn burned – I'm getting out timbers for a new one now."

(282)

"...we can make it do."

(189)

Overlooking Seven Tree Pond in South Union, this home nearly was lost; the barn was destroyed. Now it's enlarged and surrounded by flower gardens.
c. 1910, c. 1930

Perched on a ledge in South Union, this fine home is getting thoughtful and appropriate attention.
c. 1935, 2003

An old residence and part of one of South Union's foundries, this lovely home has been thoroughly renovated and restored.
2002

By the mill run in South Union, this has gotten an attractive new front. See the South Union pathways photos for a side view of this.
2003

Nicely redone and painted. Middle Road.
2003

East Union's long-time store continues to be a public building. It is now Grace Fellowship. Payson Road.
1905, 1940

Good things are happening to East Union barns. Daniels Road, Payson Road (2), Buzzell Hill Rd.
2003

A faithful reconstruction of the carriage barn now leads to a new garage. Depot Street.
2003

It is good to see a new covering of shingles on an old structure. Town House Road.
2003

This well-maintained barn has received window and foundation work recently. Shepard Hill Road.
2002

New shingles on a nice square and level little barn. Butler Road.
2003

Superbly maintained. Skidmore Road.
2003

Two barns transformed. Middle Road.
Sennebec Road.
2003

A classic, restored some years ago.
Daniels Road.
2002

Carefully nestled into the hill,
and carefully maintained.
Clarry Hill Road.
2002

Laboriously restored, this early home commands a view of spectacular mountains from Butler Road.
2003

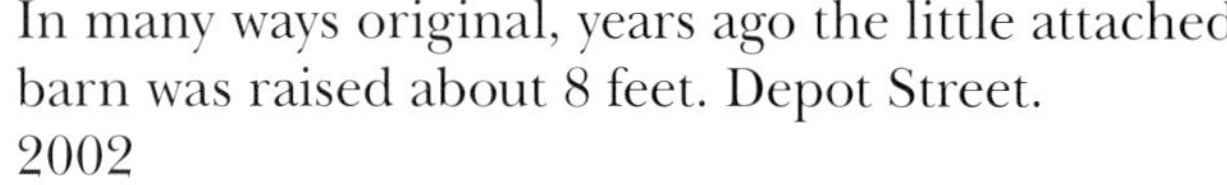

In many ways original, years ago the little attached barn was raised about 8 feet. Depot Street.
2002

An old frame modified over the years and enhanced again recently. Appleton Road. 1998, 2003

A major project carried off with very attractive results. Common Road. 2003

This photograph was taken not long after the stage and bathroom areas were added in 1888.

The Old Town House (1840 and 1888) has been restored by the Union Historical Society for the community's use. It was made a National Registry property in 2001. 2001

2001

On the National Registry of Historic Places the 18th century mill now produces milled foods. Payson Road. c. 1895, 2002

The Alden House property is listed on the National Registry, also. It includes Union's first store.
2000

The Common, Then and Now

Early on, this large home became an inn, The Rural House. It sits securely above the Common. Burkett Road.
c. 1880, 1998, 2003

Two homes on the Common continue there with new functions, a B&B and a restaurant. The Common.
c. 1890, 1900, 2002

The automobile has been tended to at Heald Highway and Appleton Road.
c. 1940, 1975, 2003

Still completely recognizable at Common Road's west end, this large building houses an ambulance service and other businesses.
c. 1965, 1965

Heald Highway's former home of Fuller Equipment has evolved to become a large, modern Agway store.
c. 1970, 2002

Rufus Gilmore's home, The Red Store, Moody's Store – this centrally located building is undergoing another rebirth. c. 1920, c. 1900, 2003

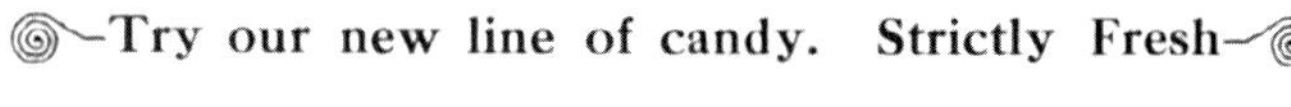

We mourn the loss of venerable buildings.
c. 1900

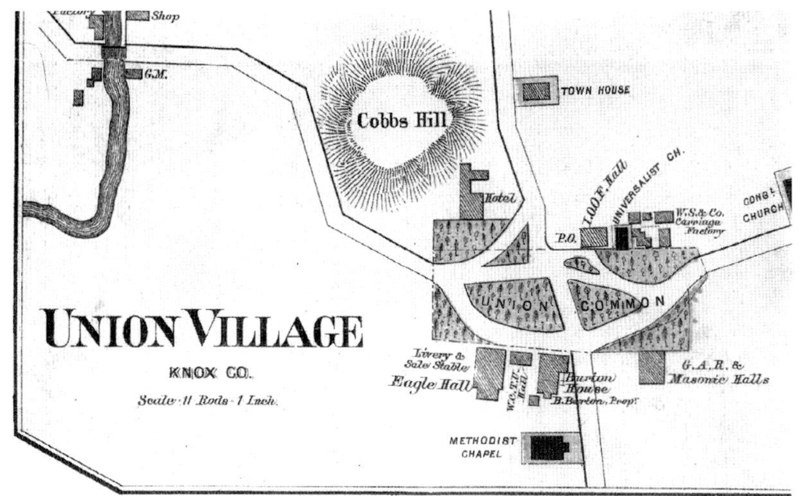

Part of a map.
1888

The early photo predates the bandstand, monument, and water trough.
c. 1875

2003

The small building at the right exists; the others are replaced. c. 1890, c. 1900, 1928

C. W. Clarke. Manufacturer of Fine Custom Harness, Union, Maine.

2003

The west side of the Common, under the elms.
c. 1900, 2000

c. 1890

2003

1890

c. 1920, c. 1955

The federal home on the right is easily seen. Look closely, too, at the only Queen Anne house in Union, with its porch intact. On the Common, Burkett Road.
c. 1910

2003

Prior to 1925, this shows two buildings that survive. Those to the right have gone through replacement after changes. The 1239 pound bell seen here may be heard ringing from the People's United Methodist Church to which it was moved.
c.1915

Rebuilt after a fire, the Masonic Hall and store. c. 1930, c.1950

The Red Store has become Moody's. There's the mileage sign.
c. 1935

2001

The old church has become tired. The coach-works, Wingate & Simmons, is at its right.
c. 1900

Several major buildings comprised the wagon works.
c. 1880

2003

The once stylish Robbins House became less so with the loss of the old barn. The Historical Society restored the house to its original Greek Revival appearance.

c. 1900

c. 1950

2003

Celebrating those who served.
1888

The elms have been replaced but the bandstand and monument continue.
c. 1900

2003

CORNET BAND.
MAINE.

1890

SEVEN TREE GRANGE

1925

50TH ANNIVERSARY
SEVEN TREE GRANGE.
UNION, ME.

Architectural Details

Photographed by Todd Caverly

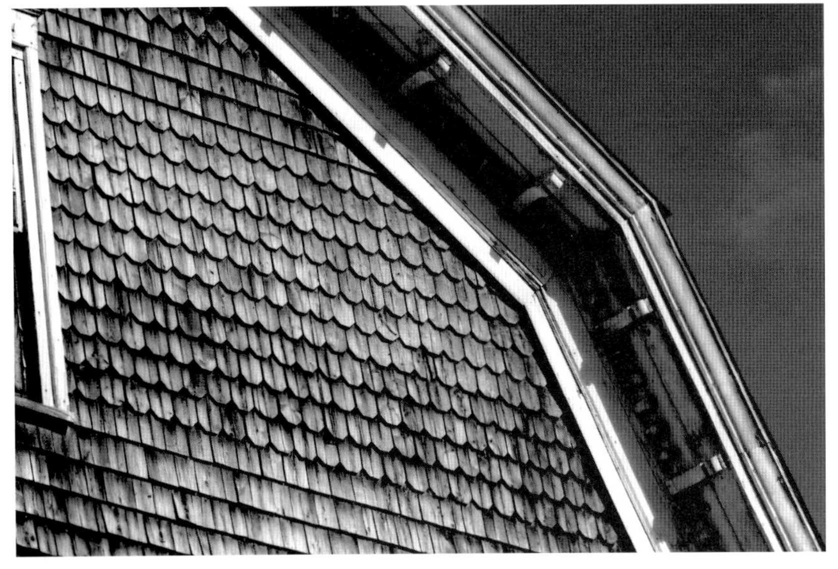

A 1917 Tour of Union Village

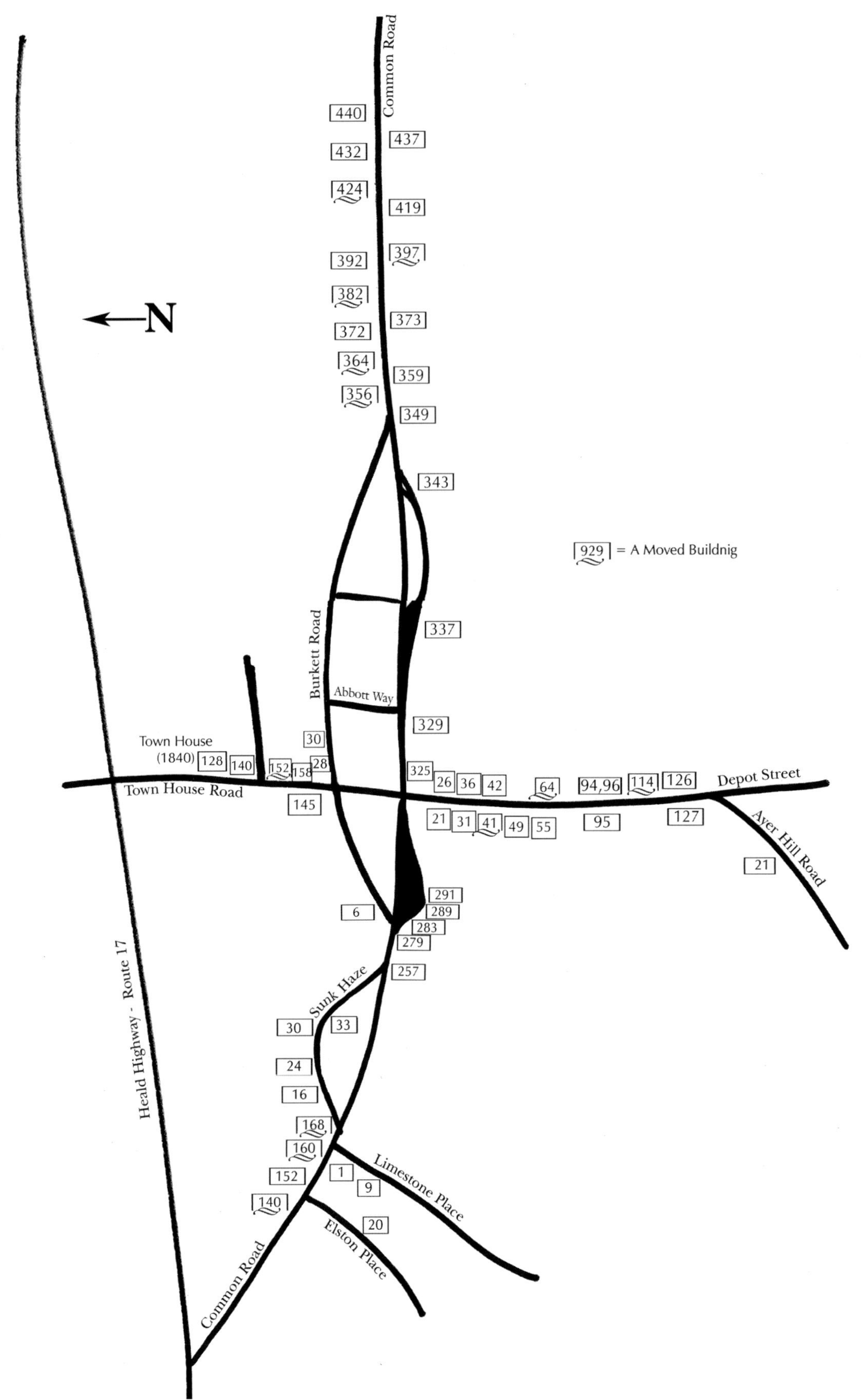

Common Road
440
437
432
424
419
397
392
382
N
373
372
364
359
356
349
343
929 = A Moved Buildnig
337
Burkett Road
Abbott Way
329
30
Town House
(1840)
128
140
152
158
28
325
26
36
42
64
94,96
114
126
Depot Street
Town House Road
145
21
31
41
49
55
95
127
Ayer Hill Road
21
291
6
289
283
279
257
Sunk Haze
30
33
Heald Highway - Route 17
24
16
168
160
1
Limestone Place
152
9
140
20
Elston Place
Common Road

List of Houses in Union by Warren Hills, written in 1917

This material might make good reading. It would make an even better tour. The addresses are our "best guess" based on what is written here, what long-time Union people recall, and reference to Matthews' *Horse and Buggy Days*. This might be called "The Dance of the Houses," since so many have been moved to their location.

---

140 Common — A Gushee house, this was built and used for a casket factory near Hills (Mills) on the western side of the river. It was bought by Isaac H. Cunningham and moved to its present location about 1869.

152 Common — Mr. William Besse's house was built by Nathan Bachelder probably around the early thirties. Mr. Besse added another story to the house.

160 Common — The C. A. Robbins (now John Cunningham) house was moved from the farm near the farm of O. N. Butler on the land now owned by Thomas Butler.

168 Common — The Gushee house, across the river, built by George Fossett, east of his store, was moved to its present location.

257 Common — The house now occupied by Mrs. Roscoe Miller was undoubtedly built for a "mill house," that is, for the man who attended the "Grist Mill," an important mill where farmers could have their grain ground. Millers in those days shared with the owners. Built in the early part of the last century, rebuilt by Roscoe Miller near the close of the century.

279, 283 Common The Robbins Block, 1896.

289 Common — Augustus Jones' house was built in 1839 by Nelson Cutler, then or subsequently a lawyer in town.

291 Common — The dwelling now owned by Conrad Seiders (Charles Howe) or family was probably built during the first years of the last century by Robert Bunting. A pound which stood on the spot where the Oddfellows' Block now stands (*until 2001*) was an annoyance to him and was removed. In the middle of the last century it was known as the "Bunting House."

325 Common — The Alonzo F. Morse house on the corner, was built by Dr. Elisha Harding, then a physician in town, not far from the year 1826.

329 Common — The next building is the Vose Block, so called. It was built by Elijah Vose in 1851 or 1852. Mr. Vose was then a lawyer in Union.

337 Common — The Congregational parsonage was built in the early years of the nineteenth century and rebuilt, also enlarged by Zuinglius Collins in the year 1855 or 1856.

343 Common	The dwelling now owned and occupied by Jason M. Robbins was built by Dr. Isaac Flitner in 1847, then a physician here and was succeeded by doctors Walker, Albee, Judkins, Varney, and Bennett.
349 Common	The Helen (Mossman) Cummings house was built by Albert Rice, a joiner of Union, in 1841.
356 Common	The Samuel Cumming's house, now owned by C. F. Lermond formerly stood on the corner where Jason (Clemice) Robbins house now stands and was moved to its present location in 1847. (*That's now 343*)
359 Common	The Frank Gordon (Alfred Hills) house was probably built by Abner Pitts, a harness maker in town, during the first half of the last century. The then basement was used as his shop. The Gordon house was rebuilt and enlarged by C. R. Dunton in 1889.
364 Common	The William Green (now Frank Creighton) house was used as a plow shop and blacksmith shop and set a few rods west of Barrett's Corner, west of the house that burned, and moved to its present location in the late forties.
372 Common	The Congregational Church was built in 1839.
373 Common	The Rev. C. R. Plumer (George Fossett) residence was built by Frank Whitten in 1894.
382 Common	Joel Hills' dwelling was formerly the ell of Gilmore's hotel, long known as the "Rural House," kept by William E. Cobb, now owned by Dura (Henry) Ames, and moved to its present location about 1840.
392 Common	The Warren Hills' house was built about 1825 or 1826 by Zacheus Litchfield, a shoemaker, who occupied it and carried on shoemaking for many years.
397 Common	The Oscar D. Gould (Charles Smith) house was moved from a spot near Samuel E. Fuller's, was rebuilt and enlarged by John Dean, a tailor, in the late fifties.
419 Common	The J. A. Hughes house was moved from a spot between McFarland's blacksmith shop (Messer Garage) and the Seider (Howe) house, and rebuilt, a1so enlarged by Henry R. Cross probably sometime during the sixtics.
424 Common	The house owned by Addie Bartlett was built for, and used for a store by Elmer Blunt on the land between the dwelling houses of Joel Hills and Warren Hills in the early forties, and moved to its present location about 1850.
432 Common	Miss Lucy Daniels' house was built about the year 1851 for Nathan D. Payson, by Christopher Young.
437 Common	The Dr. Hadley house was erected by Captain Ephriam Lovett during the late fifties.

440 Common	The house of Woodbury Carroll was built in the early part of the last century by Jacob Litchfield, a tanner, whose tan yard was on the west side of Young's Brook where O. J. Jameson's blacksmith shop now stands.
6 Burkett	The Burkett House was built by the person whose name it bears in the year 1891.
28 Burkett	The Clark (now Moody) store on the corner was built about 1838 by Eben Cobb for a dwelling for Major Rufus Gilmore. The deed of the Free Church lot states from so many "rods" from Mr. Cobb's new building.
30 Burkett	The Burkett store was built by Augustine Eastman about 1858 or 1859.
140 Town House	The Gifford dwelling next to the town house was built by Ebenezer Cobb in 1849 and occupied by him until his death.
145 Town House	The Dura (Henry) Ames house, formerly Cobb's Hotel was built in 1801 by one of the Gilmores, either Rufus or David: probably David, and used as a hotel by a Gilmore and afterwards by Eben Cobb from 1836 to 1849, and by William E. Cobb from 1849 to the time of his death.
152 Town House	The next dwelling owned now by L. L. Russell, (later by Almeda Creighton) was formerly a store standing on the spot where Mrs. Burkett's tenement house now stands. It was moved into its present location and made into a tenement house about 1875 or 1876 by Mr. Emery F. Joy. ("Tenement" has, in recent times, become a negative word; earlier it simply meant a multiple dwelling, parts of which were for rent.)
158 Town House	Mrs. Ellen Burkett's tenement house was built on the spot where her present house now stands, probably by Nathaniel Robbins.
16 Sunk Haze	The Fossett store and dwelling was built by Cyrus G. Bachelder, a trader, in 1836 and occupied by him.
24 Sunk Haze	The C. W. Post house was probably built by Joseph Vaughn and exchanged for property of Bradley R. Mowry at South Union.
30 Sunk Haze	The Judson Alden house was built by Bnj. Gallop in the first half of the last century. Mr. Gallop was a blacksmith and edged tool maker in a shop below the Grist Mill and carried on a business there.
33 Sunk Haze	The Robert Clark house, a part of it was moved to its present location by I. C. Hovey in 1847, a basement was built beneath it, and an addition made to its front and a story added.
20 Elston Lane	The John F. Fossett house was built by Llewellyn (*Lawrence?*) F. Bachelder in 1856.
1 Limestone	The Fossett (now Newbert) house across the street from the Fossett store, now occupied by Mr. Howard was built by Isaac C. Hovey, a cabinet maker in 1842. The upper part was used for a dwelling and the lower part for many years was used for the manufacture of cabinet furniture.

9 Limestone	Hezekiah Hemenway's house was built by Noah S. Rice in 1842.
21, 31 Depot	The Methodist Church was erected in 1902 and the parsonage a few years later.
26 Depot	The William Moody Robbins house was built by Isaac C. Hovey in 1848, then a cabinet maker.
36 Depot	The Mank house was built about 1849 by Micajah G. Morse, a painter of Union.
41 Depot	The John L. Bradford house, then a one story building, was built on the spot where Nathan D. Robbins (Hampton) house stands, by Abel Walker; in 1803. It was moved to its present location in 1855 or 1856 and a story added.
42 Depot	The house of Dr. H. H. Plumer was built about the year 1855 or 1856 by J. Warren Wentworth, a jeweler.
49 Depot	The Fred M. Lucas house was built by Samuel E. Kellogg in the late fifties.
55 Depot	The Harvey S. Moore house was built by Joseph O. Cobb, a harness maker, in 1861.
64 (?)Depot	The house and store on Railroad Street was built as a one story store in the early part of the last century on the spot where the Oddfellows Block now stands. (*That Block burned in 2002*) A story was added by Nelson Cutler about 1845 and was moved near its present location about 1894.
94, 96 Depot	The George Robbins tenement house known as the Syndicate Building was built by Fred E. Burkett, John Pillsbury, and Calvin I. Burrows.
95 Depot	The Mrs. Barnard (Lovejoy) or Dr. Bennett house was built by Israel R. Hills and Joseph Eastman in the fifties.
114 Depot	The Ethel S. Cummings house was built by him in 1894 on the farm of William Wagner and moved to its present location some ten years afterwards.
126 Depot	The Herbert E. Messer house was built about 1895 by Lewis Frank Andrews, now of Thomaston, (1917).
127 Depot	The A. P. Robbins house was built on the spot where dwelling of W. E. Haskell now stands (*now gone from about #40 Ayer Hill Road*) , probably in the latter part of the eighteenth century, but whether by Nathaniel Robbins or his father, Josiah Robbins, the writer never learned. It was moved to its present location some time in the first half of the nineteenth century.
21 Ayer Hill	The Walter R. Ayer house was built by Almon S. Tolman about 1873.

A *real* heroine – intelligent, tough, caring, independent – immortalized in *Come Spring.* Jemima, wife of Captain Joel Adams.

We go on as our predecessors sleep.
c. 1960

The Title

Through the Union Historical Society's newsletter and by verbal announcement, we sought suggestions for a title for this latest publication.

The original working title, from the curator's group was "Since 200 Years." That reflects the goal to publish previously unpublished images, old and new, and to provide an overview of local history since 1974, Union's bicentennial year and the date of "200 Years."

A summer resident suggested "Union: A Town with Heart." He has felt particularly welcome in Union. Another submitted "Timeline," to reflect our goal of continuing to record town history. A third idea was "Union's Recent History - Since 200 Years."

The beautiful title photograph is excellent as a picture and, at the same time, provides a symbolic "bridge." It is believed to have been taken by Linwood Moody, a long-time Union resident and writer of "The Maine Two-Footers," the story of Maine's narrow-gauge railroads. The photograph seems to reflect the sentiments of the other suggested titles.